Some of the common and uncommon

BIRDS OF
ONTARIO
AND QUEBEC

By DAVID A. HANCOCK AND JIM WOODFORD

GENERAL PUBLISHING CO. LIMITED
Don Mills, Ontario

A

B

A

B

CANADA GEESE

C

D

3

CONTENTS

BIRDS OF NORTH AMERICA SERIES: is designed and produced by HANCOCK HOUSE PUBLISHERS Saanichton, B.C. Each book in the Series is in two parts. A 48 page section deals with the general facts about birds and it appears in similar form in all Regional Editions. The second section of 20 pages which changes with each Regional Edition, deals with the specific facts about birds and birdwatching in that Region.

Copyright © 1973 David Hancock

ISBN 0-7736-0027-2

Library of Congress Catalog Card Number 73-84985

First published 1973

by GENERAL PUBLISHING CO. LIMITED

Printed in Canada

YELLOW WARBLER   A   CEDAR WAXWING   B

PART 1
ABOUT BIRDS

DISTRIBUTION

WHAT IS A BIRD?

Birds are animals with feathers, descendants of scaly reptiles that ruled the earth hundreds of millions of years ago. Archaeopteryx, the earliest known fossil bird, appears to be nothing more than a lizard with feathers. Birds still have scales on their legs. Indeed, birds were around long before birdwatchers came along to classify and enjoy them.

WHERE ARE BIRDS FOUND?

During this long period of geological time birds have evolved into many species of different shapes and sizes. They have specialized their tools for making a living and thereby adapted to many environments. Today more than 8000 bird species exist in the world. Except perhaps for the interior of Antarctica, birds occur in season over the entire earth. But some areas have poor bird fauna. These places include the polar regions and remote oceanic islands. Generally speaking, the further islands are from continental land masses, the fewer birds they have, but all islands have some birds. The largest variety of land birds inhabit temperate and sub-tropical savannah country, tropical semi-deserts and tropical forests. Two major factors control the distribution of birds. First, the number of plant species in the area affects the number of different habitats available for different birds to live in. Tropical forests with over 200 varieties of trees may house 500 bird species. Boreal forests of the north with only 10 or 12 tree species house fewer than 100 kinds of birds. The second factor is the ease by which a bird can find an area. A remote island will not often be found, particularly by birds that can't rest on water.

SPECIES DISTRIBUTION

TABLE 1. NUMBER OF SPECIES IN DIFFERENT AREAS

	TOTAL	BREEDING
Antarctica	50	16
Alberta	320	247
British Columbia	390	280
California	463	288
Canada	525	420
Florida	406	162
Manitoba	320	248
New Brunswick	318	168
Newfoundland	262	130
New York	414	222
Northwest Territories	270	185
Nova Scotia	315	161
Ontario	370	269
Oregon	362	235
Prince Edward Island	225	104
Quebec	330	229
Saskatchewan	318	240
United States (Continental)	728	538
Washington	353	235
Yukon	182	128

The *Golden Eagle* was once found throughout the world. Now in North America the bird is commonly found only in the western mountains and the northern wilderness.

A

The *Starling* is a European import that has been a very successful colonizer. In many areas it has displaced our native species by occupying all the available nesting holes.

B

CLASSIFICATION

BY THEIR BEAKS AND FEET WE SHALL KNOW THEM

OSPREY   A

Ornithologists, scientists who study birds, recognize about 165 families of living birds. Birds are sorted into their family groups by checking the tools they use to make a living. A bird's tools include its feet and beak. Not many years ago it was said you could tell a man's occupation by looking at his hands. The parallel is not so simple today when even the laborer is influenced by television to keep his hands soft and his nails well manicured. Birds are more natural. By their beaks and feet we shall know them. The sparrows and grosbeaks have short, stout bills for crushing seeds, and feet adapted for hopping on the ground or from limb to limb. Waterfowl have webbed feet for swimming and wide bills for 'shoveling' up food. Grebes, loons and herons have long, pointed bills for seizing or spearing fish. The flesh-eating hawks, falcons and owls have strong talons for holding prey, and hooked beaks for tearing meat. The chisel beaks of the woodpeckers and sapsuckers enable them to split wood and bark to get at grubs and sap. The broad, gaping bill of the flycatchers, swallows and nighthawk are ideal for scooping up insects on the wing. And so it goes, each family or species has its tools modified in a special way to facilitate its making a living.

SHARP-SHINNED HAWK   B

RING-NECKED PHEASANT A

GREATER YELLOWLEGS B

The digger	Ring-necked Pheasant
The prober	Greater Yellowlegs
The crusher	Evening Grosbeak
The chiseler	Yellow-bellied Sapsucker
The tearer	Sharp-shinned Hawk

YELLOW-BELLIED SAPSUCKER C

EVENING GROSBEAK D

FEATHERS AND FLIGHT

GREAT BLUE HERON

FLIGHT

Birds are the most mobile of earth's creatures. Wings come in many shapes and sizes and serve many purposes. Today, the Maribu Stork and the Wandering Albatross share the record for the longest wing-span — eleven feet. Bald and Golden Eagles sometimes attain a wing-span of seven feet; the Great Blue Heron (above), five and a half feet. Pheasants and Ruffed Grouse have short, broad wings which allow them a quick burst of speed to escape predators, then a short glide to settle back to earth again. The swifts' long, narrow wings enable them to stay aloft for hours, and possibly even for days at a time. Many hawks and eagles have large, broad wings permitting them to soar easily on warm rising air bubbles over land. Falcons and other bird-catching hawks have much less wing surface area allowing them to beat their wings more rapidly for faster flight, but at the expense of soaring efficiency.

Flight serves to carry birds to food, away from predators, and seasonally on migration journeys. Flight also aids in courtship. The Peregrine Falcon and the Common Snipe perform aerial displays to attract their mates. The Ruffed Grouse standing on a log beats its wings to produce a drumming sound which declares ownership of its territory. Scoters, Common Murres and penguins are capable of underwater flight.

SPEED OF FLIGHT	
Peregrine Falcon	
Diving	180 miles per hour
Level flight	60 miles per hour
Canada Goose	45 miles per hour
Mallard	55 miles per hour
Robin	30 miles per hour
Herring Gull	25 miles per hour
Starling	55 miles per hour

FEATHERS

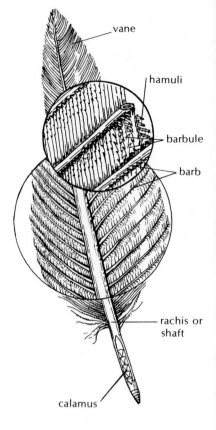

- vane
- hamuli
- barbule
- barb
- rachis or shaft
- calamus

BLACK TERN

Feathers, collectively called plumage, give protection from the physical environment and are an aid to flight. Colored feathers, or disruptive patterns can act as camouflage. A display of colorful feathers can help attract mates or repel competitors, and a brightly colored male bird can distract predators from the nesting female.

The tail feathers of woodpeckers are stiff and act as a prop against the tree. The feathers on the face of barn owls are arranged in a disc, probably aiding in picking up and focusing minute sounds on the ear bones. Many waterfowl pluck out their under coating of down feathers on the belly and use it to line their nests. The warm, bare belly skin helps to heat the eggs while the down prevents the loss of heat to the cold outside air.

SEMI-PALMATED PLOVER   A.

BALD EAGLE   B.

The *Semi-palmated Plover* (above) nests in a shallow scraping on bare ground while the *Bald Eagles* (left) build an elaborate nest 5-12 feet across in a secluded tree. The unorthodox nest of the *Robin* (below) held up construction work for three weeks.

ROBIN'S NEST IN SHOVEL   C.

BIRDS AND NESTS   THE BIG AND THE SMALL

In size, North America's birds range from the Calliope Hummingbird weighing only an eighth of an ounce, to the 38 pound Trumpeter Swan. Bald and Golden Eagles are often thought to be much heavier than they really are. The males weigh between 5 and 7 pounds; the females between 8 and 12 pounds. Since they can lift and carry only about one quarter of their weight there is little truth in the old wives' tales about eagles carrying off lambs and calves — that is unless you have a herd of 2 pound cows! The heaviest birds in the world are the Ostrich and Emu, which have sacrificed their ability to fly.

TRUMPETER SWAN A

CALLIOPE HUMMINGBIRD B

NESTS

Bird nests vary greatly in size and structure. Cowbirds and cuckoos avoid the chores of nest building and parenthood altogether, by laying their eggs in someone else's nest. The foster parent then does all the work. Oystercatchers, Nighthawks, and Peregrine Falcons make no nest or simply lay their eggs in a shallow scraping in the gravel.

Woodpeckers chisel out nest cavities in trees, which in turn are used by an assortment of other birds — bluebirds, Tree Swallows, Wood Ducks and Starlings. Warblers and vireos make elaborate nests lined with down, hair, the gossamer of willows, and often camouflaged with lichens.

The function of a nest is to offer protection for the eggs and developing young. Tufted Puffins, which nest in deep burrows on remote islands and spend most of their life out on the open ocean where there are few predators, get by with laying just one egg. The Ruffed Grouse and the Pheasant which nest exposed on the ground and are eaten by many predators — hawks, skunks and man — lay many eggs. And, as with most ground nesting birds, the young are precocial. That is, they are able to get up and move around to feed and avoid enemies as soon as they hatch. In contrast, the young Bald Eagle doesn't leave the nest until it is fully grown and able to fly at the age of 10½ weeks.

13

MIGRATION

SNOW GEESE A

Migration is any regular movement between two areas brought about by changes in environmental conditions. In North America, seasonal migrations usually follow a north and south direction. Some birds perform seasonal migrations even within the tropics. Others are wanderers, moving with the wet and dry seasons which determine their food supplies.

There is no one answer to account for the migration of birds. Nature, however, abhors a vacuum. In summer vast areas of the frozen north thaw, and temporarily become suitable homes for birds. Insects, seeds and other foods become abundant, and birds, because they are mobile, move in. Only a few species like the Gyr Falcon and the ptarmigan that the falcons live on are adapted to the rigors of the northern winters. The Arctic Tern may travel 30,000 miles over North America and South America to Africa, and back to the north to breed. Daily migrations are movements to and from feeding areas and roosts. Generally speaking, large birds migrate by day; smaller ones by night when they can avoid the predators. Birds such as cranes and hawks fly by day in order to take advantage of the rising hot air bubbles. By circling over a rising air mass they gain height, then glide for miles to the next thermal. In mountainous country there are altitudinal migrations. During spring melt, birds move from their winter habitat in the valleys to higher elevations as nesting sites and food become available.

FLOCK OF SANDERLINGS B

SPOTTED SANDPIPER A

BIRD SOCIETY

Most birds are sociable, at least seasonally, though some hawks, owls and woodpeckers live singly except during the breeding season. Robins, ducks and sandpipers gather in flocks during migration but form into pairs for the breeding season when they are intolerant of others of their own kind and sex. Gulls and sea birds, on the other hand, form into loosely associated groups only during winter, but in summer they congregate into highly organized colonies to breed. These different social systems aid in survival. Sea birds spend most of the year widely dispersed over the open oceans, but for nesting require isolated islands free of land predators. These specialized requirements force sea birds to congregate on a few suitable islands, making sociability a necessity. Although colony nesting birds often appear to nest without any order there is, in fact, a minimum distance of a foot or so between each nest. This is the pecking reach of each bird and it assures some privacy and space to each pair. On the other hand, Song Sparrows and Cooper's Hawks defend considerably larger territories. This ensures that a minimal food supply is exclusively theirs. The gathering of birds into colonies makes it easier for them to find mates, coordinate their breeding activities and cumulatively defend their nests. A disadvantage is the disturbance of many birds at one time by pleasure boaters and vandals.

RING-BILLED GULL B

PART 2 BIRD GROUPS

LOONS AND GREBES

Loons sit low in the water, propel themselves underwater with webbed feet to catch fish and never emerge onto land except to nest. The *Common Loon* is famed for its yodel-like laugh.

Grebes are weak flying, tailless water birds with lobed toes.

A
THE EGGS

B
THE FIRST CHICK

C
THE DEPARTURE

PIED-BILLED GREBE

HORNED GREBE   A

COMMON LOON   B

MALLARD AT SUNSET A

247 kinds of waterfowl occupy the world, some 63 species being found in North America. All members of this order are adapted for life in the water. They have webbing between their 3 front toes, and flattened bills with tooth-like edges that act as strainers. Most species are strong flyers undertaking long migration flights between breeding areas in the north to wintering areas in the south. The young are down-covered and can walk and swim a few hours after hatching.

B
MUTE SWAN

SNOW GOOSE   A

MALLARD WITH BROOD   B

BUFFLEHEAD A

BLUE-WINGED TEAL B

PHEASANT [
RING-NECKED PHEASANT
A scratching bird

RUDDY DUCK C

WIDGEON D

20

DEFIANT PEREGRINE FALCON   A

PEREGRINE FALCON EYRIE   B

DIURNAL PREDATORS

HAWKS, FALCONS, AND EAGLES

All birds, for at least part of their lives, live on other animals and therefore are predators. Usually, however, predators are considered as either diurnal — the daytime hunters such as the hawks, falcons and eagles, or nocturnal — the night-time hunters such as owls. The diurnal hunters are some of the most colorful, spectacular and yet least understood of any birds. The beautiful *Peregrine Falcon* is an endangered species because it has been unjustly shot, driven from its breeding grounds by encroaching human activities and had its food (and consequently itself) poisoned by pesticides.

PEREGRINE FALCON AND
DAY OLD CHICK

ADULT BALD EAGLE   A

RED-TAILED HAWK   B

LARGE PREDATORS

Predator size is definitely not the only criterion in determining prey size. Our largest eagle, the *Bald Eagle,* feeds primarily on small fish or carcasses of dead animals. The *Turkey Vulture* feeds exclusively on carrion.

However, the 8-12 pound *Golden Eagle* is an active predator and can kill jack rabbits, marmots and even foxes. The *Osprey* has scaly toes and sharp talons especially suited for catching fish. The Red-tailed Hawks, along with the other broad-winged soaring hawks, are often unjustly blamed for raiding barnyards. These soaring hawks are often seen around farms hunting their main prey of mice, rats, snakes, and insects.

GOLDEN EAGLE   A

OSPREY OR FISH HAWK   C

TURKEY VULTURE   B

25

LESSER PREDATORS

In most birds of prey the male and female look alike, though the females are always larger. The *Sharp-shinned* (page 8), *Cooper* and *Merlin* are strictly bird-catching hawks that occasionally become a nuisance around bird feeders, however, the unnatural concentration of prey around feeders is a very natural attraction to a predator. If plenty of brush cover is provided the feeding birds will not be unfairly exposed to predators. The delicately built *Marsh Hawk* and *Kestrel* are rodent and insect feeders.

ROUGH-LEGGED HAWK   A

COOPER HAWK   B

BANDED SHARP-SHINNED HAWK   C

MERLIN   D

ADULT MALE KESTREL A

KESTREL AT NEST HOLE B

MARSH HAWK C

HERONS, BITTERNS, RAILS, AND COOT

Herons and *bitterns* are long necked and legged birds that frequent waterways and feed on aquatic life. They both fly with their necks folded back as opposed to the cranes and geese that keep the neck outstretched during flight. Also frequenting marshes but unrelated to the above group are the *rails* and *coot*. While the coot is commonly seen along pond and lake shores either bobbing down to pull up submerged vegetation or grazing along the bordering lawns, the rails are secretive birds only seen by close examination of dense marsh vegetation.

GREAT BLUE HERON   A

AMERICAN BITTERN   B

VIRGINIA RAIL A

COOT WITH EGGS B

COOT WITH YOUNG C

AMERICAN BITTERN D

SORA RAIL E

29

BONAPARTE'S
GULL
C

GULLS, TERNS AND SHOREBIRDS

This diverse group of birds also includes the true sea birds. Most birds of this order have long pointed wings and either long legs or webbed feet. They are mainly riparian, or water frequenting, and many undertake long migrations.

HERRING GULL EATING CARP   A

HERRING GULL CHICK   B

PECTORAL SANDPIPER   E

SOLITARY SANDPIPER   D

30

RUDDY TURNSTONE   A

BLACK-BELLIED PLOVER   B

DOUBLE-CRESTED CORMORANT   A   Nests in scattered colonies in lakes.

CORMORANT AND DOVE

MOURNING DOVE   B

OWLS

YOUNG SAW-WHET OWL
WITH MOUSE

NIGHTWATCHERS: THE OWLS

YOUNG HORNED OWLS   A

HORNED OWLS   B

No group of birds more elicits a feeling of comradeship, empathy or respect than owls. Their wise expression comes from the fact that their eyes are fixed in their sockets. The owl must turn its head to focus on an object, thus giving the appearance of 100 percent attention and concentration. All owls fly silently to aid in hearing their prey and in approaching it. The leading edges of their flight feathers are supple and soft so they make no noise rubbing together or against the air.

HORNED OWL BROODING YOUNG   C

SCREECH OWLS BRINGING FOOD TO YOUNG   A

The *Horned Owl,* or Tiger of the Woods (previous 2 pages), and his smaller cousin the *Screech Owl,* nest very successfully around farms or in towns. Most owls eat mice, rats and rabbits, though many of the smaller owls also consume great quantities of insects. Generally nocturnal in habit, the *Snowy Owl* of the north and the local *Short-eared Owl* do considerable hunting by daylight or at dusk.

BARRED OWL   B

SHORT-EARED OWL   A

LONG-EARED OWL   B

37

NIGHTHAWK AND KINGFISHER

NIGHTHAWK AND YOUNG   A

WOODPECKER

DOWNY WOODPECKER

YOUNG BELTED KINGFISHERS   B

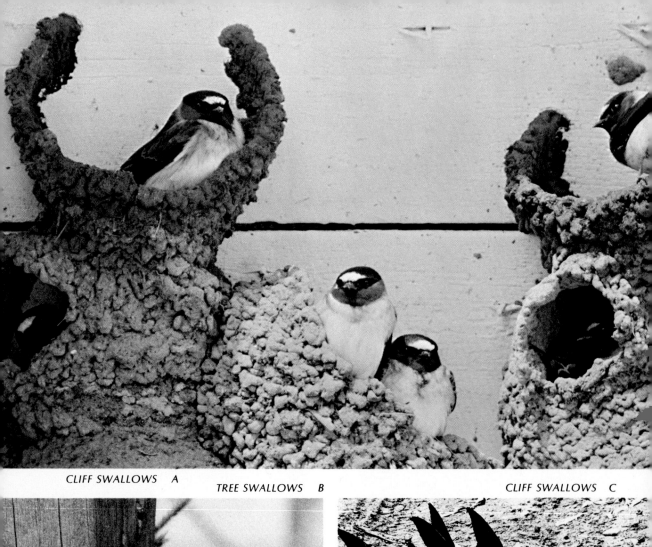

CLIFF SWALLOWS   A

TREE SWALLOWS   B

CLIFF SWALLOWS   C

TREE SWALLOWS   D

40

BARN SWALLOWS A

BANK SWALLOWS B

CROW C

PERCHING BIRDS

These two and the next six pages deal with the perching birds, or passerines. They constitute by far the largest and most diverse group of birds and present the greatest challenge for identification.

SWALLOWS

Elegant, beneficial, graceful, bold or beautiful — few birds more qualify for compliments than the diminutive swallows. All have long pointed wings, usually a forked or notched tail, small weak feet and a wide gaping bill for snatching up insects on the wing. The group is adapted to living under many circumstances, nesting in tree holes, rock cavities, or with a mud nest stuck to cliffs or buildings.

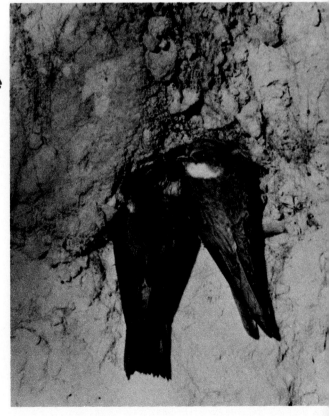

HORNED LARK   B

GOLDEN-CROWNED KINGLET
CAUGHT ON BURDOCK   A

RED-EYED VIREO   C

LEAST FLYCATCHER   A

WOOD PEWEE   C

WHITE-BREASTED NUTHATCH   B

ALBINO ROBIN   A

LOGGERHEAD SHRIKE   B

HOUSE WREN   C

YELLOW THROAT A

WILSON'S WARBLER B

MAGNOLIA WARBLER C

ORANGE-CROWNED WARBLER D

CATBIRD E

AMERICAN GOLDFINCH A

MEADOWLARK B

46

FOX SPARROW   B

CHIPPING SPARROW   C

WHITE-THROATED SPARROW   A

PURPLE FINCH   E

GRASSHOPPER SPARROW   D

PART 3 BIRD WATCHING AND MORE

Bird watching is a disease. It can strike quickly and without regard to age or sex. According to recent surveys there are over 12,000,000 birdwatchers in North America — truly a disease of epidemic proportions. But why? The answer is simple. Birds are everywhere from the back yard to wilderness areas of every continent. Their diversity of size, shape, color and behavior offer exciting challenges for indoor or outdoor recreation. Birdwatching can be a private interlude in the day, a social gathering, a science or a business through the sale of your stories or photographs of birds.

How photograph at left was taken — not all bird photography requires long waits in blinds.
Some owls, like the *Saw-whet Owl,* can be approached quite closely in the daytime for close-up photographs. While the owls can see perfectly well in daylight they often prefer to sit tight rather than fly and risk the wrath of crows.

KILLDEER PLOVER

SAW-WHET OWL   A

In fact, bird watching is big business. More books are devoted to the birds than any other field of natural history. Hundreds of millions of dollars are spent annually on automobiles, motels and travel tours directly by people pursuing birds. Cameras, binoculars, telescopes and tape recorder sales to birders contribute even more. And the manufacture of bird feeders and sale of bird food supports thousands of persons.

Good binoculars and an easy to use field guide are the essential tools for the birdwatcher. However, disease can cause fever and irrational behavior and this I suspect is the reason so many birders stumble into the woods armed with extra check lists, cameras and a multiple of lenses, and tape recorders with parabolic reflectors. The following is a brief introduction to the hardware of birdwatching.

FIELD GUIDES

A good field guide contains clear illustrations of the birds for easy identification, a range map to quickly tell when and where the bird is likely to be, and a brief description of the bird's behavior, habitat, and easily identifiable characteristics. Nothing more need be said than GET:

Birds of North America by Robbins, Bruun, Zim and Singer. Golden Press. Hard or soft bound.
Or the slightly less efficient and more costly two volume series:

Field Guide to the Birds of Eastern N.A. and Field Guide to the Birds of Western N.A. by R. T. Peterson. Houghton Mifflin Co.

48

BIRD CHECK LISTS

Check lists are simply a local (city) or regional compilation of all birds found in the area concerned (see page 66). They are made of stiff card for carrying in the pocket or field guide. They usually state whether a bird is commonly or rarely seen and at what season. Most Natural History Clubs make these available to visiting birders free of charge or 10 to 15 cents each. They make it easy to record the day's sightings and form a permanent record. Get them for the areas you visit.

PHOTOGRAPHY BLIND

BINOCULARS

These come in a wide range of quality, price and power. Don't get a magnification of more than 6, 7, or 8 power. It's impossible to hold more powerful ones steady under perfect conditions, let alone after running 100 yards through the woods after a 'new bird'. For the untried beginner many excellent, yet heavier weight pairs, can be purchased for 20 to 50 dollars. Avoid the 200 to 300 dollar pairs. Recent advances in optics and light-weight bodies such as the Nikon ultra-compact prism binoculars bring quality, durability and light weight for 60 to 90 dollars. The above come in a magnification of 6, 7 or 8.

Scopes are a specialist's tools, requiring more investment and a good tripod to mount them on. Forget this implement until your binoculars are well used.

PHOTOGRAPHY

Without proper care bird photography can become the most malignant outgrowth of birding, draining dollars, time and the spouse's patience. On the other hand, the ultimate challenge to seeing a new bird or exciting behavior is to record it on film for later reference, or for friends, business or science. The photographs of this book come almost exclusively from amateur birder-naturalists. And why not make an enjoyable hobby pay its way?

There are two important features in bird photography. First, you must know the habits of your subjects. That is, know where to go and to look for them; to be able to predict their behavior patterns and to understand their tolerances to your disturbance. Once you have found out where a bird is likely to appear, then only patient waiting (often from the seclusion of a blind) is required to capture exciting moments on film. That is, provided you thoroughly understand the second important feature of photography — the operation of your camera and film. There are dozens of good camera makes and models highly suitable for bird photography. Unfortunately, many camera stores give advice dependent upon the availability of stock and the discount that they make on selling. Below are some general and specific recommendations that suit this photographer. First, get a reflex camera — where you look through the lens to see exactly what is being photographed and whether it is in focus. Second, the 35mm format is most flexible for optional lenses and attachments, is light-weight to carry, is simple and quick to use, and is economical to keep fed with film. Two basic lenses will take 99

HORNED OWL

percent of your pictures. First is a Macro lens with a nearly normal focal length 50-55mm. The macro lens permits pictures to be taken within one foot. This is particularly important if you are out birding and want a close-up of a bee, flower or nest. Oh, you're not interested in insects and flowers? Well, the birds are and most birders quickly develop an appreciation of all nature. The second lens I recommend you get is a telephoto of moderate length — 150 to 200 mm. This can be hand held at 125th of a second to give flexibility for 'opportunistic' photography. That is, getting a picture whenever you can. This is opposed to setting up the equipment in a blind, possibly with strobe lights and a super abundance of patience. A large telephoto of 400 to 500mm is a seldom used frill that can come much, much later.

In wildlife photography it is often desirable to change lenses quickly to get a shot of a fleeting subject. Here a bayonet mount on the lens is helpful. Also, go the few extra dollars and get a through-the-lens meter or even a fully automatic camera. This eliminates worrying about a separate meter getting wet, banged or lost, or of remembering to take it with you or use it. The through-the-lens meter is always there and its one or two faults are more easily corrected than in a separate meter. The camera manufacturer will outline another 101 features of his product, but most are quite insignificant to general or bird photography. Here we are speaking of a camera and lens in the 300 or 400 dollar range. This is a minimum outlay for new equipment though the same second hand items can be acquired

EASTERN BLUEBIRD   A   *HAIRY WOODPECKER   B*

for one third to one half price. In fact, 500 dollars will give you a new outfit with the two lenses. The accommodating shop clerk will be pleased to throw in a free roll of film knowing he has another birder hooked. The new Minolta or Pentax 35mm camera wraps up all the above features with durability and lightness of weight — again an important consideration. By the time you have tramped 10 hours with your left pocket bulging with field guide, check list and a few chocolate bars; the right pocket full of film and an extra lens; your binoculars around your neck; the camera over your shoulder or mounted on a tripod across your shoulder, you are conscious of each extra ounce. When at the last moment you decide to leave the lunch at home in order to carry an extra lens you know you are thoroughly initiated as a bird-photographer — a hungry but happy one.

SOUND RECORDING

Recording bird song was a specialist's hobby that has become popular and practical by the development of high quality Cassette Recorders for under 100 dollars. A birder in Toronto, Canada, Dan Gibson, has developed a portable reflector which weighs less than three and a half pounds and has a frequency response to 15,000 cycles. It is now feasible for the weekend naturalist to record professional quality wildlife sound to elaborate his slide talks or sound his movies. Movies! ! Oh, oh, I had hoped to avoid mentioning that category. Learn well 35mm still photography before you even consider movies. The quality of 8mm movies is simply too disappointing for the effort. Super 8 is better, but once bitten by the bug you won't be satisfied until you have 16mm. The camera and lenses will begin at 1200 dollars. Add a good tripod — the key to good movies — and you set out another 500 dollars — yes, 500 dollars for the tripod alone. And film — if you only shoot four times the amount of film that ends up in your final production, and that is a very good ratio for wildlife footage, you will have about 20 dollars worth of film per viewing minute — that's 1200 dollars per hour. But this cheap method means running the original film through a projector where it's going to get scratched and no longer saleable. That's taboo. So you have a copy made before you even view the processed film — another 600 to 800 dollars, please. Then you add . . . please start your photography with 35mm slides, then if your banker is friendly, think of movies.

PART 4 BIRDING IN ONTARIO AND QUEBEC

WHIMBREL A

By Jim Woodford

Ontario and Quebec make up about one-third of Canada, with a total of 1,007,442 square miles. Both are dominated by the Boreal Forest which covers about four-fifths of the land mass. It is estimated that 350 million pairs of wood warblers nest in this forest. Agriculture and progress have so obliterated any trace of the natural Carolinian and Alleghanian Zones that it is more convenient to think of them as a combined Southern Hardwood Zone. Both provinces have extensive coastlines — Ontario on the Great Lakes; Quebec on the Atlantic; and both share the shores of James and Hudson Bays.

There are over one million square miles to cover and therefore this guide will provide just the briefest introduction to the region and a few details about the best birding areas, as well as references to further information.

BROWN THRASHER B

ONTARIO

Ontario stretches a thousand miles from east to west and one thousand and fifty miles from north to south. Southern deciduous forest occurs in a narrow belt along Lake Erie and the west end of Lake Ontario. To the north along Hudson Bay there is a corridor of true tundra. And in between there is a mosaic of 250,000 lakes, rivers, forest — the Canadian Shield. Ontario offers great variety to the student of nature; prickly pear cactus grows in the south, polar bears roam in the north.

Winter is a good time to begin birding in Ontario. While there are fewer species present, there is usually a good variety to provide the beginner with a 'field course' in bird identification. Many species of waterfowl winter along the Great Lakes and the Niagara River; hawks and owls are found in open, farm areas; winter finches like Redpolls, Pine Siskins, crossbills, and grosbeaks are common forest species; and bird feeders attract chickadees, nuthatches, Cardinals, Blue Jays, and others.

A highlight of the birder's year is the annual Christmas bird count held in a two-week period during the Christmas season. The combined total for southern Ontario is usually 120-140 species and about 300,000 individual birds. (See page 65)

GREAT GRAY OWL C

YELLOW-BELLIED FLYCATCHER D

Spring comes early for the Ontario birder. Horned Larks arrive back from the south in February, the harbingers of a steady stream of migrants that lasts until mid June. Fall also begins early, as migrant shorebirds may be seen by mid July. May is the best month for observing migrants, the peak in southern Ontario is about May 10. Early morning is the best time to see and hear these southern arrivals and many bird clubs sponsor a series of May walks.

For further, more detailed information the fine book *A Naturalist's Guide to Ontario* edited by W. W. Judd and J. M. Speirs is highly recommended.

Now let us look at some of the best birding spots in Ontario.

PILEATED WOODPECKER A

RUFFED GROUSE B

MAP OF ONTARIO AND QUEBEC

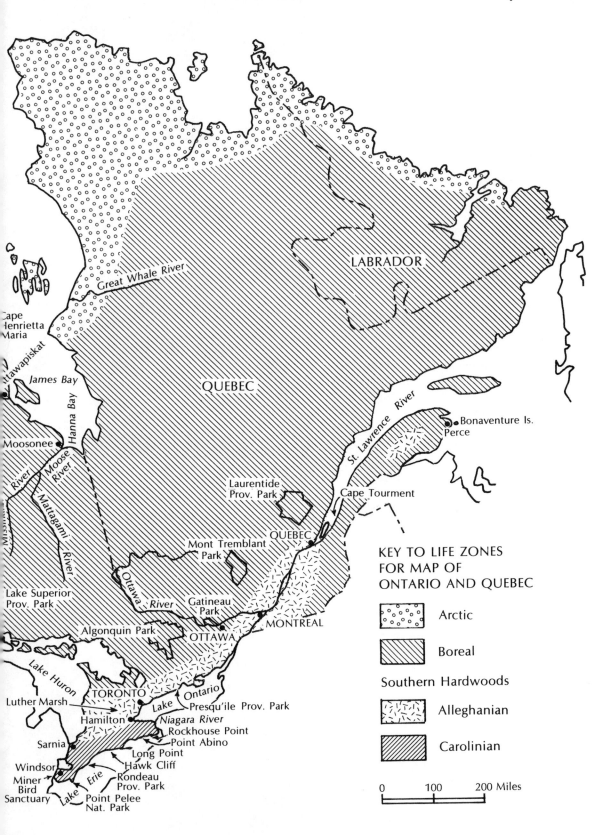

LABRADOR

QUEBEC

Great Whale River

Cape
Henrietta
Maria

Attawapiskat

James Bay

Hanna Bay

Moosonee

Moose
River

River

Mattagami
River

NELSON

Lake Superior
Prov. Park

Ottawa
River

Laurentide
Prov. Park

Mont Tremblant
Park

QUEBEC

Cape Tourment

Bonaventure Is.
Perce

St. Lawrence River

Algonquin Park

Gatineau
Park

OTTAWA

MONTREAL

Lake Huron

Luther Marsh

TORONTO

Ontario

Hamilton

Lake

Presqu'ile Prov. Park

Sarnia

Niagara River
Rockhouse Point
Point Abino
Long Point
Hawk Cliff
Rondeau
Prov. Park

Windsor

Miner
Bird
Sanctuary

Lake

Erie

Point Pelee
Nat. Park

KEY TO LIFE ZONES
FOR MAP OF
ONTARIO AND QUEBEC

Arctic

Boreal

Southern Hardwoods

Alleghanian

Carolinian

0   100   200 Miles

SOUTHERN ONTARIO

This region has the richest fauna of any part of Ontario, reflecting the diversity of habitats available.

MINER BIRD SANCTUARY

You may witness one of Ontario's most impressive gatherings of geese at the Miner ponds located about three miles west and south of Kingsville. April and October through December are the best months.

POINT PELEE NATIONAL PARK

If there is a birders' shrine in Canada, it is Point Pelee. There is nothing quite like a May morning on the Point. You may see over 100 species of birds; perhaps twenty-five to thirty of these being warblers. May is the best time to visit Pelee for the spring migration; May 12 is about the peak of movement. October and September are best for the spectacular fall hawk migrations. Point Pelee is south of Leamington, and is the southernmost point of the mainland of Canada. The National Parks Service operates an excellent nature center and will provide bird lists and information.

RONDEAU PROVINCIAL PARK

Rondeau is one of the best examples of southern deciduous woodland in Canada. It is a good migration area in May and September. Long ponds between raised beaches offer nesting sites for such rarities

LUTHER MARSH

One of the best spots to see marsh birds and waterfowl; Luther Marsh is located about thirty miles from Kitchener. This is an extensive marsh where Redhead, Ruddy, Gadwell and many other more common duck species breed. This marsh also houses one of the largest heronries in the province, with nesting Green, Great Blue, and Night Herons, as well as American and Cattle Egrets. A canoe is essential to see much of this area.

BLUE GOOSE   A

BLACK AND WHITE WARBLER   B

as Prothonotary Warblers, Acadian Flycatchers and Louisiana Waterthrushes. The beaches are noted for shorebird concentrations and there is an extensive marsh. These are located south of Blenheim on Highway 3.

SANDHILL CRANE   C

HAWK CLIFF

To reach Hawk Cliff take a southerly route from St. Thomas on Highway 4 to Union, then turn east for one and one-quarter miles and then turn right to the lakeshore. At Hawk Cliff it is possible to see more hawks in one day than any other place in North America. Broadwings are the most common, a peak number of 70,000 was seen on September 16, 1961. About 16 species may be seen at the Cliff and peak

BROAD-WINGED HAWK A

flights generally occur between September 10 to September 23.

LONG POINT

The Bay is famous as a stop-over for migrating waterfowl, especially Whistling Swans. The best observation period is from mid March to late April. Other species, such as Canvasbacks and Redheads are also common. Long Point is a twenty mile sand-spit sticking out into the middle of Lake Erie. It is accessible only by boat or a four-wheel drive vehicle. Canada's largest bird banding and passerine bird research station is located at the tip of the Point.

For information write: Long Point Bird Observatory, 116 Three Valleys Drive, Don Mills.

ROCKHOUSE POINT AND POINT ABINO

The shoreline of Lake Erie from Fort Erie west is one of the finest areas to observe migrant shorebirds from mid July to October. The best plan is to follow the road along the shore and stop at every opportunity to scan the shoreline.

FRANKLIN'S GULL B

NIAGARA RIVER

This famed river is a great spot to observe diving ducks, grebes and gulls, and of course, terns. Look for Forster's, Caspian and Black Terns; Bonaparte's, Little and Franklin's Gulls; and occasional rarities such as the Kittiwake. A winter drive along the River from Niagara-on-the-Lake to Fort Erie often produces some surprises.

PRESQU'ILE PROVINCIAL PARK

Located south of Brighton, Presqu'ile offers a good variety of habitats; a fine marsh, beaches, and mudflats as well as offshore islands used as nesting grounds by gulls and terns.

COMMON TERN C

COMMON TERN D

COMMON TERN E

SHARP-TAILED GROUSE   A

SPRUCE GROUSE   UPLAND PLOVER   C
B

ALGONQUIN PROVINCIAL PARK

Algonquin is Ontario's second largest park, 2,700 square miles. Its high altitude gives it a colder climate and more northern fauna and flora. In summer the earnest birder may turn up Ravens, Gray Jays, Olive-sided Flycatchers, Boreal Chickadees, Spruce Grouse, Blackbacked Three-toed Woodpeckers, Evening Grosbeaks, and many more. A winter visit is often rewarding with large flocks of winter finches along the highway and trails (take snowshoes!). The Ontario Ministry of Natural Resources has a fine park museum and staff naturalists will supply checklists and information.

LAKE SUPERIOR PROVINCIAL PARK

Found north of Sault Ste. Marie, the park offers beautiful shoreline scenery. Many of the species listed above for Algonquin may be found in this park.

NORTHERN ONTARIO

The major difficulty to birding in northern Ontario is access. There are dozens of good areas, but getting to them may be difficult and expensive. There is now a series of provincial parks along Highway 11 and these afford the traveller opportunities to sample northern Ontario birds. Canoe trips along northern rivers may be exciting and provide sightings of breeding birds such as Golden Eagles and Peregrine Falcons, which are seldom seen in the southern part of the province. Farther north Winisk Park and the Attawapiskat and Moose river areas are recommended. Information on these and others is available from the Ministry of Natural Resources, Parliament Buildings, Toronto, Ontario.

LONG-TAILED JAEGER   D

RED-THROATED LOON   E

PINTAIL   F

GYR FALCON   A

SNOWY OWL   B
GOS HAWK   C

GOLDEN PLOVER   D

GRAY JAY   E

MOOSONEE

This tidewater community is reached by the Polar Bear Express train from Cochrane. White-crowned and Fox Sparrows nest here. Palm and Orange-crowned Warblers sometimes are found, though sparingly. In spring and fall, spectacular numbers of waterfowl and shorebirds gather on the famous lowlands near the mouth of the Moose River and up the coast. Shipsands Island is one of the best observation points. Hannah Bay is a staging area for Blue Geese. It is possible to arrange travel by aircraft or canoe at Moosonee. Contact the local Ministry of Natural Resources office.

CAPE HENRIETTA MARIA — POLAR BEAR PROVINCIAL PARK

This is Ontario's largest park and is found at the junction of James and Hudson Bays. There is a breeding colony of Blue and Snow Geese near Kwinabiskak Lake. Polar Bear Park is accessible only by boat or aircraft. It affords the Ontario birder an opportunity to sample the Arctic in their own province. King Eiders, Dunlins, Pectoral, Stilt, and Semipalmated Sandpipers, Golden Plovers, Northern Phalaropes, Parasitic Jaegers and Lapland Longspurs have all been found nesting in the Park. Gyr Falcons and Snowy Owls are common visitors that may eventually be found nesting in the Park.

59

BLACK-CAPPED CHICKADEE   A

QUEBEC

Quebec is the largest of Canada's provinces, stretching 1,200 miles from the international boundary to Cape Childlay on Hudson Strait. Nearly 71,000 square miles are covered by lakes and rivers and 160,000 square miles are covered with dwarf forest and tundra. Quebec has more than 5,000 miles of coastline and the magnificent St. Lawrence River traverses much of the southern region.

Bird study here has never enjoyed the popularity it does elsewhere in Canada, but some of the most spectacular North American sights of birding, such as the Gannets of Bonaventure Island and the Snow Geese of Cap Tourments are to be seen in this area.

RUBY-THROATED HUMMINGBIRD   B

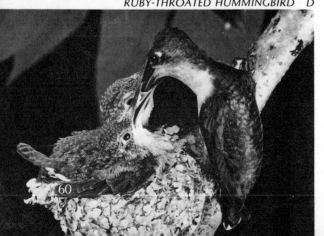

RUBY-THROATED HUMMINGBIRD   C

RUBY-THROATED HUMMINGBIRD   D

SNOWY OWL   F

SWAINSON'S THRUSH   E

CHESTNUT-SIDED WARBLER
A

ARCTIC TERN B

RED-HEADED
WOODPECKER C

CAP TOURMENTS

This stopover point for Snow Geese is located some thirty miles east of Quebec City. Earl Godfrey in *Birds of Canada* suggests that the whole population of the subspecies *atlantica* stops over here, possibly 50,000 individuals. In fall, the first Snows arrive about mid September and their numbers continue to increase until mid October. Spring arrival is late March and the birds remain until early May.

MONT TREMBLANT PARK

Mont Tremblant is a large park with a variety of habitats and is located about seventy-five miles north of Montreal. It offers the birder an opportunity to observe many

species of warbler, loon, thrush, and sparrow on their breeding grounds. There are also birds like the Boreal Chickadee, Raven, Three-toed Woodpecker and Spruce and Ruffed Grouse feeding here.

ST. LAWRENCE RIVER

There are good birding spots all along the St. Lawrence where one may see waterfowl, shorebirds, various species of gull, and terns. Closer to the mouth, seabirds may sometimes be seen. A trip along the north shore takes the birder through some varied country, climaxed by some tundra-like areas near Sept-Iles which houses many characteristically northern birds. We recommend late June and July.

COMMON GRACKLE   D

CHIMNEY SWIFT   E

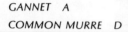

GANNET A   GANNET B   GANNET C

COMMON MURRE D

BONAVENTURE AND PERCE

Bonaventure Island is famous throughout North America for its nesting Gannets and other seabirds. It is reached by boat from the village of Percé. It is estimated that between 7,000 and 10,000 Gannets nest in this area. To reach the nesting cliffs you must walk across the island. Some of the Gan-

COMMON MURRE   E

COMMON MURRE   F

BLACK GUILLEMOT   A   BLACK GUILLEMOT   B   RAZORBILL   C

COMMON PUFFIN   E.

nets nest on top of cliffs, which if climbed afford excellent views and numerous opportunities for photography. Other species you may chance to see include Common Puffins, kittiwakes, Razor-billed Auks, Common Murres, Black Guillemots and Herring Gulls. Many other species occur on the island and in the island woods.

COMMON PUFFIN   D

NORTHERN PHALAROPE   F   WHITE-WINGED SCOTER   G

LAURENTIDE PROVINCIAL PARK

This park is situated in the Boreal Forest region of Canada and is an excellent place to see and hear nesting warblers. It has been estimated that there is one pair of nesting warblers per acre of forest! Species include Black-throated Green, Bay-breasted, Cape May, Tennessee, Magnolia and Blackburnian Warblers. Kinglets and thrushes are also to be spied here.

WHIMBREL   A

GRAY-CHEEKED THRUSH   B

MAGNOLIA WARBLER   C

KNOW MORE ABOUT THE BIRDS

CLUBS TO JOIN

THE CANADIAN NATURE FEDERATION, 46 Elgin Street, Ottawa. KIP 5K6 (613 233-3486) Publishes *Nature Canada*, operates a book store and coordinates activities of Natural History and Bird Clubs across Canada

FEDERATION OF ONTARIO NATURALISTS, 1262 Don Mills Rd. Don Mills, Ont. (416 444-8419) Coordinates more than fifty local bird and nature clubs, publshes *Ontario Naturalist*, a newsletter and operates a bookstore.

HAMILTON NATURALISTS CLUB
P.O. Box 384,
Hamilton, Ont.

KINGSTON FIELD NATURALISTS
Box 831,
Kingston, Ont.

LONG POINT BIRD OBSERVATORY
116 Three Valleys Drive,
Don Mills, Ontario.

MCILWRAITH FIELD NATURALISTS
834 Dufferin Av.,
London, Ont.

OTTAWA FIELD NATURALISTS CLUB
Box 3264, Postal Station C,
Ottawa, Ont.

SOUTH PEEL NATURALISTS CLUB
Box 91,
Port Credit, Ont.

THUNDER BAY FIELD NATURALISTS CLUB
15 Knight Street,
Thunder Bay "P" Ont.

TORONTO FIELD NATURALISTS CLUB
49 Craighurst Av.
Toronto 12, Ont.

TORONTO ORNITHOLOGICAL CLUB
2056 Breezy Brae Dr.,
Port Credit, Ontario

THE PROVINCE OF QUEBEC SOCIETY FOR THE PROTECTION OF BIRDS
c/o Miss M. H. Robertson,
83 Holoton Av.
Westmount, Quebec.

LE CLUB DES ORNITHOLOGUES DE QUEBEC, INC.
8191 Avenue du Zoo,
Orsainville 7, P.Q.

LA FEDERATION QUEBECOISE DE LA FAUNE—QUEBEC WILDLIFE FEDERATION
a/s M. Paul E. Pageau,
6424 Rue St. Denis,
Montreal, P.Q.

THE MASSAWIPPI BIRD CLUB
c/o Dr. J. K. Lowther,
Bishop's University
Lennoxville, Que.

REFERENCES

Breeding Birds of Ontario by James L. Baillie and Paul Harrington. (out of print but available in libraries)

Birds of Simcoe County by O. E. Devitt	$2.75
History of the Birds of Kingston by Helen R. Quilliam	$4.95
Ontario Birds by L. L. Snyder	
Oiseaux du Quebec by Jean Bedard	
Birds of the Labrador Peninsula and Adjacent Areas by W. E. C. Todd	$22.50
Birds of the Ungava Peninsula by Francis Harper	$2.00
Birds of Canada by Godfrey. A National Museum of Canada publication (Les Oiseaux du Canada)	$15.00
Birds of North America, A Field Guide to Identification by Robbins, Brunn, Zim and Singer	$4.50 soft
	$7.50 hard
A Field Guide to the Birds by Roger Tory Peterson	$4.50 soft
	$6.95 hard
Birds of the Eastern Forest (Volume 1) by Lansdowne & Livingston	$20.00
Birds of the Eastern Forest (Volume 2) by Lansdowne & Livingston	$22.50
Birds of the Northern Forest by Lansdowne & Livingston	$20.00
Ducks, Geese and Swans of North America by Kortwright	$9.50

A CHECK LIST OF BIRDS OF ONTARIO AND QUEBEC

British Columbia; Alberta, Saskatchewan and Manitoba; and the Atlantic Provinces; (and 21 U.S.A. Regional Lists), are all available on stiff card for carrying in pocket.   15 cards — $2.00

Most of the books listed above are available from your local book seller or all the books and check lists are available from:

HANCOCK HOUSE PUBLISHERS
3215 Island View Road,
Saanichton, B.C., Canada

AUDUBON CHRISTMAS BIRD COUNTS FOR ONTARIO AND QUEBEC 1972-73

LOCATION	SPECIES	BIRDS	COUNTERS	COMMENT
Grenville-Hawkesbury, Que.	38	1716	14	clear, 25°-25°, calm wind
Hudson, Que.	29	2511	28	snowstorm, 5°-10°, visibility poor
Hull-Ottawa, Que., Ont.	68	11709	82	clear, -4° - -13°, snow cover
Lac Rouillard, Que.	7	63	5	light clouds, -15° - 5°, lakes frozen
Lennoxville, Que.	32	2976	24	lakes frozen, rivers open, 26°-37°
Low, Que.	27	406	2	overcast, 30°-33°, snow cover
Montreal, Que.	32	3998	29	cloudy AM, clear PM, 0°-3°
Quebec, Que.	36	3020	23	36 in., snow cover, 16°-25°, abundant ice fields
Trois-Rivières, Que.	22	872	25	cloudy AM, 20°-30°, clear PM, calm
Bancroft, Ont.	14	257	2	clear AM, cloudy PM, 15°-26°
Barrie, Ont.	45	2656	9	overcast and foggy, 32°-42°
Belleville, Ont.	24	1468	10	cloudy, 15°-20°, 8 in. snow cover, river open
Blenheim, Ont.	90	12,457	22	overcast, 32°-24°, light snow
Carleton Place, Ont.	30	1144	26	snow all day, 5°-16°, lakes frozen
Deep River, Ont.	31	1215	19	overcast, snow, lakes frozen
Dryden, Ont.	20	605	15	cloudy to sunny, 12°-22°
Guelph, Ont.	43	4598	30	freezing rain, overcast, 30°-37°
Hamilton, Ont.	87	58,000	23	clear, 7°-22°, snow cover, harbor open
Kettle Point, Ont.	62	5669	29	overcast, 35°-40°, snow cover
Kingston, Ont.	83	8875	48	sun AM, overcast PM, snow cover
Kitchener, Ont.	47	5139	27	fresh snow, rivers open
London, Ont.	72	4632	24	heavy snow, blowing, 21°-23°
Long Point, Ont.	91	11,873	25	cloudy, 20°-26°, visibility poor
Manitoulin, Ont.	29	1181	10	clear AM, cloudy PM, 1°-13° snow
Meadford, Ont.	50	3543	21	snow cover, drifting, 20°-30°
Minden, Ont.	23	776	9	clear, snow cover, -10°-10°
Moscow, Ont.	28	1972	12	cloudy, 21°-31°, cone crop good
Napanee Falls, Ont.	36	2820	14	rain, cloudy, 10°-16°
Niagara Falls, Ont.	71	33,669	28	drizzle, light snow, water pools, 34°-36°
Oshawa, Ont.	65	7650	16	rain, ponds open, 20°-35°
Owen Sound, Ont.	48	3275	22	rivers in flood, 40°-50°
Peel-Halton Counties, Ont.	80	10,793	43	sunny, snow cover, 20-25
Peterborough Ont.	35	2455	21	clear, windy, ponds frozen
Pickering Township Ont.	76	11,502	22	overcast, green patches, 32°-36°
Point Pelee, Ont.	71	3891	13	light snow, ponds frozen, 40°-43°
Port Hope-Cobourg, Ont.	49	4191	18	snow, lake open, 20°-30°
Presqu'ile Provincial Park Ont.	48	3818	15	variable snow cover, 30°-35°
Richmond Hill, Ont.	50	4818	44	freezing rain, overcast, 24°-34°
St. Thomas, Ont.	73	11949	15	cloudy, snow cover, 30°-35°
Sault St. Marie Ont., Mich.	33	972	26	cloudy, snow and ice in bay; 0°-15°
Thunder Bay, Ont.	31	4421	18	snow, water frozen, 5°-19°
Toronto, Ont.	84	17,631	38	wet snow, creeks open
Westport, Ont.	30	1,232	12	overcast, 16°-35°
Wiarton, Ont.	35	1465	14	rain, lakes frozen, 25°-40°
Woodhouse Township, Ont.	69	5608	18	wet and swampy, 29°-33°

CHECK LIST OF BIRDS OF ONTARIO AND QUEBEC

The taxonomy and nomenclature follow that of Godfrey *The Birds of Canada* 1966.

Common Loon
Arctic Loon
Red-throated Loon
Red-necked Grebe
Horned Grebe
Western Grebe
Pied-billed Grebe
Yellow-nosed Albatross
Northern Fulmar
Greater Shearwater
Sooty Shearwater
Black-capped Petrel
Leach's Petrel
Harcourt's Petrel
Wilson's Petrel
White Pelican
Gannet
Great Cormorant
Double-crested Cormorant
Anhinga
Magnificent Frigatebird
Great Blue Heron
Green Heron
Little Blue Heron
Cattle Egret
Common Egret
Snowy Egret
Louisiana Heron
Black-crowned Night Heron
Yellow-crowned Night Heron
Least Bittern
American Bittern

Wood Ibis
Glossy Ibis
White Ibis
Mute Swan
Whistling Swan
Trumpeter Swan
Canada Goose
Brant
  (incl. Black Brant)
Barnacle Goose
White-fronted Goose
Snow Goose
  (incl. Blue Goose)
Ross's Goose
Fulvous Tree Duck
Mallard
Black Duck
Gadwall
Pintail
Green-winged Teal
Blue-winged Teal
Cinnamon Teal
European Widgeon
American Widgeon
Shoveler
Wood Duck
Redhead
Ring-necked Duck
Canvasback
Greater Scaup
Lesser Scaup
Common Goldeneye

Barrow's Goldeneye
Bufflehead
Oldsqaw
Harlequin Duck
Steller's Eider
Common Eider
King Eider
White-winged Scoter
Surf Scoter
Common Scoter
Ruddy Duck
Hooded Merganser
Common Merganser
Red-breasted Merganser
Smew
Turkey Vulture
Black Vulture
Swallow-tailed Kite
Goshawk
Sharp-shinned Hawk
Cooper's Hawk
Red-tailed Hawk
  (incl. Harlan's Hawk)
Red-shouldered Hawk
Broad-winged Hawk
Swainson's Hawk
Rough-legged Hawk
Ferruginous Hawk
Golden Eagle
Bald Eagle
Marsh Hawk
Osprey
Crested Caracara
Gyrfalcon
Peregrine Falcon
Pigeon Hawk
Sparrow Hawk
Spruce Grouse
Ruffed Grouse
Willow Ptarmigan
Rock Ptarmigan
Greater Prairie Chicken
Sharp-tailed Grouse
Bobwhite
Ring-necked Pheasant
Gray Partridge
Turkey
Whooping Crane
Sandhill Crane
King Rail
Virginia Rail

Sora
Yellow Rail
Purple Gallinule
Common Gallinule
American Coot
American Oystercatcher
Lapwing
Semipalmated Plover
Piping Plover
Snowy Plover
Killdeer
Ruddy Turnstone
American Woodcock
Common Snipe
Long-billed Curlew
Whimbrel
Eskimo Curlew
Upland Plover
Spotted Sandpiper
Solitary Sandpiper
Willet
Greater Yellowlegs
Lesser Yellowlegs
Knot
Purple Sandpiper
Pectoral Sandpiper
White-rumped Sandpiper
Baird's Sandpiper
Least Sandpiper
Curlew Sandpiper
Dunlin
Short-billed Dowitcher
Long-billed Dowitcher
Stilt Sandpiper
Semipalmated Sandpiper
Western Sandpiper
Buff-breasted Sandpiper
Marbled Godwit
Hudsonian Godwit
Ruff
Sanderling
American Avocet
Red Phalarope
Wilson's Phalarope
Northern Phalarope
Pomarine Jaeger
Parasitic Jaeger
Glaucous Gull
Iceland Gull
Great Black-backed Gull
Herring Gull

Ring-billed Gull	Acadian Flycatcher	Warbling Vireo	Pine Grosbeak
Black-headed Gull	Traill's Flycatcher	Black-and-white Warbler	Common Redpoll
Laughing Gull	Least Flycatcher	Prothonotary Warbler	Pine Siskin
Franklin's Gull	Eastern Wood Pewee	Golden-winged warbler	American Goldfinch
Bonaparte's Gull	Olive-sided Flycatcher	Blue-winged Warbler	Red Crossbill
Little Gull	Horned Lark	Tennessee Warbler	White-winged Crossbill
Black-legged Kittiwake	Tree Swallow	Nashville Warbler	Rufous-sided Towhee
Forster's Tern	Bank Swallow	Parula Warbler	Savannah Sparrow
Common Tern	Rough-winged Swallow	Yellow Warbler	Grasshopper Sparrow
Arctic Tern	Barn Swallow	Magnolia Warbler	Le Conte's Sparrow
Caspian Tern	Cliff Swallow	Cape May Warbler	Henslow's Sparrow
Black Tern	Cave Swallow	Black-throated Blue Warbler	Sharp-tailed Sparrow
Razorbill	Purple Martin	Myrtle Warbler	Vesper Sparrow
Common Murre	Gray Jay	Black-throated Green Warbler	Lark Sparrow
Thick-billed Murre	Blue Jay	Cerulean Warbler	Slate-colored Junco
Dovekie	Steller's Jay	Blackburnian Warbler	Tree Sparrow
Black Guillemot	Black-billed Magpie	Chestnut-sided Warbler	Chipping Sparrow
Ancient Murrelet	Common Raven	Bay-breasted Warbler	Clay-colored Sparrow
Common Puffin	Common Crow	Blackpoll Warbler	Field Sparrow
Rock Dove	Black-capped Chickadee	Pine Warbler	Harris's Sparrow
Mourning Dove	Tufted Titmouse	Kirtland's Warbler	White-crowned Sparrow
Yellow-billed Cuckoo	White-breasted Nuthatch	Prairie Warbler	White-throated Sparrow
Black-billed Cuckoo	Red-breasted Nuthatch	Palm Warbler	Fox Sparrow
Barn Owl	Brown Creeper	Ovenbird	Lincoln's Sparrow
Great Horned Owl	House Wren	Northern Waterthrush	Swamp Sparrow
Snowy Owl	Winter Wren	Louisiana Waterthrush	Song Sparrow
Hawk Owl	Bewick's Wren	Connecticut Warbler	Lapland Longspur
Burrowing Owl	Carolina Wren	Mourning Warbler	Snow Bunting
Barred Owl	Long-billed Marsh Wren	Common Yellowthroat	
Spotted Owl	Short-billed Marsh Wren	Hooded Warbler	
Great Gray Owl	Northern Mockingbird	Wilson's Warbler	
Short-eared Owl	Catbird	Canada Warbler	
Boreal Owl	Brown Thrasher	American Redstart	
Saw-whet Owl	American Robin	House Sparrow	
Chuck-will's-widow	Varied Thrush	Bobolink	
Whip-poor-will	Wood Thrush	Eastern Meadowlark	
Common Nighthawk	Hermit Thrush	Western Meadowlark	
Black Swift	Swainson's Thrush	Yellow-headed blackbird	
Chimney Swift	Gray-cheeked Thrush	Red-winged Blackbird	
Ruby-throated Hummingbird	Veery	Orchard Oriole	
Belted Kingfisher	Eastern Bluebird	Baltimore Oriole	
Yellow-shafted Flicker	Mountain Bluebird	Rusty Blackbird	
Pileated Woodpecker	Wheatear	Brewer's Blackbird	
Red-bellied Woodpecker	Blue-gray Gnatcatcher	Common Grackle	
Red-headed Woodpecker	Golden-crowned Kinglet	Brown-headed Cowbird	
Lewis's Woodpecker	Ruby-crowned Kinglet	Western Tanager	
Yellow-bellied Sapsucker	Water Pipit	Scarlet Tanager	
Black-backed Three-toed Woodpecker	Cedar Waxwing	Summer Tanager	
Northern Three-toed Woodpecker	Northern Shrike	Cardinal	
Eastern Kingbird	Loggerhead Shrike	Rose-breasted Grosbeak	
Western Kingbird	Common Starling	Blue Grosbeak	
Great Crested Flycatcher	White-eyed Vireo	Indigo Bunting	
Eastern Phoebe	Yellow-throated Vireo	Evening Grosbeak	
Yellow-bellied Flycatcher	Solitary Vireo	Purple Finch	
	Red-eyed Vireo		
	Philadelphia Vireo		

INDEX TO SPECIES

PHOTOGRAPH CREDITS

Vic Crich 12c, 17a, 28b, 30a, 41b, 42a, 44a, 45c, 60a, 62a,b,c; J. L. Frund 30d, 44c, 47c,e; R. E. Gehlert 27a; Woodrow Goopaster 60c,d; Tom Hall 2, 3, 7a, 10, 19b,c, 20b, 29c, 40c, 51, 56c, 59c; Eric Hosking 8a, 16b, 16a,b,c, 19a, 20a, 25a,c, 30e, 53a, 57c,d, 57e, 58d, 61d, 62d,e, 63a,b,f; Edgar T. Jones 9d, 15a, 31a,b, 33, 36f, 45d; Gary R. Jones 8b, 11, 20c, 44b, 59b; K. Morck 5a, 6, 16b, 28a, 37a, 43a,b,c; D. Muir 7b, 13b, 17b, 26d, 27b,c, 29b,d,e, 32b, 34, 36b,c, 36a,b,c,d,e, 37b, 38a, 39, 40b,d, 41c,43d, 45e, 46b, 47a, 53b,c,d, 54a, 54b, 56b, 57a, 58a, 58c,e,f, 59a, 59e, 60b,e, 61a,b,e, 64a,b,c; Dr. George K. Peck 9a,b, 29a, 40a, 42b,c, 45a,b, 46a, 47b,d, 59d, 63d; Barry Ranford 63c, 63e; Chris Rees 24b; W. S. Tripp 18a, 21, 35a; Richard Wright 13a, 20b, 56a; Tom Willock 57b.